# Spiritual Fitn

## Workbook

*A guide to manage your emotions, understand their messages, clearing unwanted patterns for the last time while turning wounds into Wisdom*

By Candace van Dell

# Table of Contents

Intro............................................................3

Part 1: Return to the Authentic Self..................8

Worksheet 1 - Get Honest...............................11
Worksheet 2 - Boundaries..............................13
Worksheet 3- Desire vs. Belief........................16

Part 2: Emotional Healing...............................22

Worksheet 4 - Feel it to Heal it.......................25
Worksheet 5 - Forgiveness work......................28
Worksheet 6 - Trust & Surrender.....................32

Part 3: Transformation...................................41

Worksheet 7 - Daily Practice..........................43
Worksheet 8 - Raising your Vibration..............45
Worksheet 9 - Oneness..................................47

www.candacevandell.com
www.youtube.com/user/candacevandell

# Welcome!

This workbook is my invitation to your self realization. As you learn to turn inward, you will allow your soul to be deeply heard. By acknowledging and hearing our emotions we clear the path for inner guidance to lead us. This connection is something I can't put into words, it is a love we all crave and completely deserve.

After years of seeking and studying numerous spiritual teachings and never finding the answers I craved, I turned inward and that is when my true self was finally discovered and my inner wisdom was deeply heard. As we get honest about our authentic feelings they begin to reveal profound truths and meaning. I call this "the wise guide inside".

After years as a professional coach & healer I put the basics of my teachings into this very easy and quick study guide I call "Spiritual Fitness". You can do this work at your own pace. I explain what an emotion is, where it comes from, why it is sometimes negative and how to shift this at any moment.

Our emotions are responsible for the patterns we have in our lives. If our emotion never gets the unconditional love it needs, it never truly gets healed.  When this occurs, the unhealed emotion remains within us and expresses itself through painful patterns in our lives. This continuous pattern attempts to get our attention, be heard and healed.  We can do this when we listen to what it has to tell us without judgment.

I provide tools and daily practices that assist you in immediate relief, clarity and mastery of your patterns and emotional intelligence.

By the end of this book, self trust will be explored and your inner guidance will begin to soar. You too can become the master of your emotions and awaken to self realization.  Aligning with your True Self, is the key to your emotional health.

This book is perfect for anyone who is going through a life transition, heartbreak, quarter life crisis, identity crisis, frequent negative emotion or self doubt.  If you keep seeing the same patterns pop up in your relationships, it is mandatory that you learn to listen to the message within the pattern.  Everything is happening for us but we often think it is happening to us.  Each emotion and pattern has a message to help you regain personal power and internal joy.

This book is also for those of you, like myself who are passionate about self realization, the universe, law of attraction and may be energetically sensitive. If you wish to understand yourself, your life and how you can partner up with the universe, this book is your key to an intimate relationship with the voice of your soul.

In this workbook you will learn how to interpret and master your emotions. As energetically sensitive people we are deeply effected by the way we FEEL. At times we feel like our emotions run our lives or we ignore them completely. When we run away from our emotions, try to numb them or give them too much power, they become louder. When this occurs, we can get lost within the chaos and confusion and feel like they take over our lives, or we can shut down completely and just not feel. NONE of these coping mechanisms will work.

Our emotions always have a message for us. Our feelings are our souls GPS but we must give them boundaries and structure. When we start to understand WHAT our emotions are we can start to put them in their proper place and see that they are the doorway to our higher self. By listening to the messages we hear we can begin to steer our ship into calm and peaceful waters.

This workbook is organized into 3 very specific and necessary parts. In Part 1 you will learn about the nature of your emotions and have some important questions answered. What are emotions? Why do I have negative emotions and how do I heal and clear them? How do I set boundaries? What are my true Desire's and Belief's and how do they play a major role in my emotions?

After we answer these clarifying questions we jump into the self healing. Thats right, we heal our emotions by feeling our emotions. This part is both tricky and enlightening as we become the neutral observer of our experience.

In part 2 you will learn life changing skills and strategies. You will learn to feel it and heal it. You will learn about forgiveness work and how it is your new best friend. You will learn and experience a deeper trust and surrender. You will align with the wise guide who has always lived inside.

In Part 3 you will create a daily practice to nurture your new understanding and transform it into a KNOWING. You will learn daily exercises that anchor your higher knowing into your daily life. You will learn about your vibration and how your outer experience is a reflection of your inner reality. When your inner reality is cleaned up so is your outer experience. Lastly you will see how you have the power in each encounter. How you relate to the issue IS the issue and how you relate to YOURSELF is dictating your emotional health.

I am honored to share with you the tools and wisdom that have come from my life's journey and work. My wish is that they will forever transform your reality as they continue to transform mine and bring endless Miracles of Inner Peace and Freedom.

*"No one can tell you how to feed your soul like your soul. Listen to it. ~ Curtis Tyrone Jones*

# Part 1

## Return to the Authentic Self

# SOUL GPS (What are emotions)

If you believe that you are a divine being having a human experience then you can accept that your feelings are your souls gps.

We are currently living in an emotional dark age. No one teaches emotional intelligence in school. We are not taught how to nurture, acknowledge or clear any of our emotions, let alone understand them. Many of us grow up not dealing with them and try not to feel them. There are other people who go so deeply into them that you become lost within the chaotic expression. There are also those of us who judge what we feel and deny what is actually real.

In this first exercise you will be getting HONEST about how you feel. Perhaps for the first time you will have "in to me you see" intimacy with your own soul. The goal of this workbook is to assist you in understanding your emotions in a new way and working WITH them. When we do this our emotional "issues" / life "issues" dissolve right before our very eyes.

When we talk to our emotions as if they are a separate part of us we can see clearly and begin to transcend the potential pain, insecurity, fear or drama. We see that we are not our emotions but they are a part of us. When we master this, we can start coaching ourselves through anything and everything in a fast and efficient way.

*"Fear will disappear when we become spiritually clear" ~ Candace van Dell*

# WORKSHEET 1
## Get Honest
## Identify the Emotion

What is the "issue" or situation that caused me to feel upset? How do I feel?

......................................................................
......................................................................
......................................................................
.........

Keep in mind that I don't want to know how you think you should feel. I also don't want you to worry about how CRAZY you think it is to feel the way that you feel. I simply want to know honestly HOW YOU FEEL. This is how we get real instead of ideal.

When I think about this issue do I feel it in my body? if so, where? Heart, head, stomach, throat, etc. ?

......................................................................
......................................................................
......................................................................

When our emotions don't get released they stay stagnant in our body. Your body is always giving you signs but we often don't know how to read them. Is your pain in your throat?  Do you need to speak up?  Is it in your stomach?  Are you feeling powerless?  Is it in your head?  Are you thinking too much or in an incorrect way?  Is the pain in your heart?  Have you closed off to your own self love?  Where is the pain?  Once you establish that you can talk to that part of yourself.  If you haven't found pain in your body don't worry, don't push it.

Now that you have identified your emotion, you can be real about it and continue to heal.

Ask the sensation how you can serve it.  Hear what it does or does not tell you and thank yourself for acknowledging yourself.

*"Illness or pain is just an extension of negative emotion. When you are no longer feeling any resistance to it, it's a non-issue". ~ Abraham*

# WORKSHEET 2
## Boundaries
## Ideal vs. Real

How do you feel as opposed to how you think you SHOULD feel?

When we hold judgment about our emotions we are telling them that they are WRONG or bad or unworthy of being exactly as they are.

Your emotions are your souls gps so if you tell your emotions that they are wrong or not perfect just as they authentically are, you are in essence saying that to yourself about yourself.

Write down the ways you judge your feelings or have in the past. "It's not ok to feel this way because" ....
………………………………………………………………………..
………………………………………………………………………..
………………………………………………………………………..

Now write down WHY that is not actually true. Tell yourself now exactly why it is actually OK to feel exactly the way you do and why. If you still think it is NOT ok to feel the way you feel then you have more work to do on the above question..... go deeper!

..................................................................
..................................................................
..................................................................
..................................................................

BTW, the reason WHY it is ok to feel how you feel is because that is how you feel, period! We don't need to explain why we feel the way we feel. That would be like a baby explaining why it is hungry when it is hungry. It just is and it needs to eat when it feels hungry. Your emotions need to be acknowledged when they come up and given the attention they deserve.

Write down the ways you currently express your emotions when they come up and what the sensation feels like. An example is "I feel overwhelmed and when this happens I isolate myself" or "I get angry and find someone to be my target". When you feel _____ You do _____.

..................................................................
..................................................................
..................................................................
..................................................................

Take a look at your current "go to" coping mechanism. You may have a few different ones. Please write down the ways they serve you. Are these ways beneficial to you or destructive? How? When I feel _____ I _____.

………………………………………………………………………
………………………………………………………………………
………………………………………………………………………
………………………………………………………………………

Are you getting the results you want? Do you feel better after you deal with your emotions this way?

………………………………………………………………………
………………………………………………………………………
………………………………………………………………………

What can you do instead that is more empowering? How are you giving your power away? How could you take more responsibility?

………………………………………………………………………
………………………………………………………………………
………………………………………………………………………

# WORKSHEET 3
## Desire vs. Belief
### Negative Emotion

*"Negative emotion always means the same thing, every single time . . . my thought or behavior is moving in opposition with who I really am and what I really want. ~ Abraham Hicks*

Do you experience a pattern of negative emotion? Do you "always" go through this? An example is if you always find yourself in a similar situation in different relationships or work environments. If so write down the scenario. An example is "I always find myself in a relationship where my boyfriend/ girlfriend cheats on me. This makes me feel like _____ and the way I deal with that feeling is by _____".

................................................................
................................................................
................................................................
................................................................
............

What did THEY do and how did it make YOU feel?

...............................................................................
...............................................................................
...............................................................................
...............................................................................
..............

When they do this or trigger this emotion, what does that MEAN about you? All emotions become negative when they have a false or negative belief about ourselves or life attached to them. So when this happens and you feel this way, what does that MEAN about you? When we identify the "meaning" we have attached to it, we can see how the "meaning" was created by our own mind. The "meaning" is what creates the state of our negative emotion. An example is "When my boyfriend/ girlfriend cheats on me, it means I am worthless." You feel worthless because you have attached "meaning" to an action. If I told you that your boyfriend/ girlfriend cheated on you and there was no reason why they did that, what would you feel? We feel worthless or not good enough because we have a belief attached to WHY. It sounds like this, "they cheated and that means I am worthless." Try to write down a similar scenario that pertains to your situation. This happened _____ and I feel this way _____ because to me that thing that happened must mean this _____ about me.

..............................................................
..............................................................
..............................................................
..............................................................
..............
..............................................................
....

A false belief is anything that does not support the fact that you are a DIVINE being having a human experience. At your core you are worthy and whole.

Let's talk about the root of negative emotion a little further. When you have a desire and your thoughts are not completely and deeply in support of that desire there is an emotional DISCONNECT. There are two competing parts of you. You have a desire but then have a "fear" thought that is not in alignment with the belief in your own desire. You are not in alignment with what you want. When your thoughts are not in support of who you truly are or what you want you will experience NEGATIVE EMOTION. We clear this negative emotion by identifying WHY you are not able to fully believe in yourself or your desire. What are your limiting beliefs? An example is if you want to make a million dollars but you don't believe that this is possible. Write down some of your limiting beliefs around what you ultimately WANT. Also write down WHY you think you might be unworthy.

..............................................................
..............................................................
..............................................................
...........

Is this limiting belief true? Look for evidence that it is true. You might find that life shows you what you believe rather than what is TRUE. This is why I always say that we must believe in order to receive. The universe will give you what you tell it you believe. Try to go back into one of those scenarios and see how it could be different if you had a shift in perception.

1. Are you looking at evidence? What is the evidence that what you want may not be possible?

..............................................................
..............................................................
..............................................................
...........

2. What would you need to SEE in order to BELIEVE that it is possible?

..............................................................
..............................................................

..................................................................
...........

3. Your outer reality has not caught up with your desires therefore you need to visualize it more often and with positive emotion. The universe is made up of energy and works on momentum. Sometimes we hold a limiting belief for a long time. When we change that belief it may take the universe a little while to catch up. This is how we build trust and surrender. You may still come up against situations in your life that test your old belief system. Write down what it would look like and feel like to have your desired situation right now.

..................................................................
..................................................................
..................................................................
..................................................................
..............

Now that you have identified the issues, desired emotions and emotional judgments you are probably feeling slightly more clear. Just acknowledging ourselves with more awareness can make us feel better.

Now we can bring it all together and look at HOW important our belief is in our desire. We can also see how patterns are occurring in our lives just to reflect to us the strongest "belief" that we currently hold or have held.

When we look for evidence that an old limiting belief is true by "attaching meaning" to a situation, we are recreating that pattern in our lives.

Your homework is to look at an old situation that brings up old beliefs and emotions. Notice the emotion and choose a different and new one in the same old scenario. See how liberating it is to see how you can change your own emotion and life outcome by choosing to attach a new meaning to an old situation.

*"Most people do not see their Beliefs. Instead, their beliefs tell them what they see. This is the simple difference between clarity and confusion". ~ Matt Kahn*

# Part 2

## Emotional Healing

## FEEL it to HEAL it

This is the part where you will learn some new skills and fast tools to begin to control your own emotional state. The first key is to understand that your emotions are the part of you that need more understanding, more patience and more love, not less. When we try to gloss over our emotions they may become louder. When our emotions are not getting attention or a good release, they will also start to control us more.

I like to look at our emotions like they are little kids who desperately need our attention. If a little child does not get what it needs or wants when they need or want it, they do not just be quiet and go away. They get louder and louder until you pay attention. Your emotions act the same way. Do you ever notice how you can have a feeling about something but decide not to acknowledge it or act on it. Time goes by and the feeling gets stronger until you finally say something or do something about it. If you would just acknowledge it right away by simply saying "I hear you", you would be building a trust with your inner guidance.

Often when I start working with a new client I do the "trust" exercise and I find many times that our own inner guidance becomes very stubborn. It is as if the little child wont let you in because you ignored him or her for too long. This can take time but once you gain the trust of your inner guidance, your emotions will become your closest ally.

# WORKSHEET 4
## End Unwanted Patterns

Now you are ready to think about a recent time when you were really upset about something. Has this type of situation happened before? Make sure it is something that has been a patterned emotion for you. An example of this is "some guy cut me off on the road today and swore at me. I felt an overwhelming frustration. This "reminds" me of when _____ happened. Close your eyes, put one hand on your heart and one on your stomach.

These are two very powerful energy centers in the body. Visualize the recent situation and how you felt. Then look at the time previous to that which it reminds you of. Follow that feeling back to as many similar situations it reminds you of and write them down.

..................................................................
..................................................................
..................................................................

..................................................................
.....................................

When you get to the last time you can remember, it is time to talk with that feeling. You will keep your eyes closed and tell your feeling "I see you", " I feel you", "you are safe within me", "I am ready to hear you" in support of a deeper truth.

Be aware of any resistance to open. Also be aware of any sensations in your body. Lastly be aware of any visions or messages your emotion has for you.

With your eyes still closed, thank your emotions for letting you in or showing you where they are at with you.

Now you will look at the first time this emotion was ever triggered. When was it? How old were you? Focus on that period back in time and ask your emotion what "conclusion" you drew about the situation. The emotion you are still having to this day in similar situations is because of the "conclusion" you drew about what was happening the first time it ever occurred.

This is similar to the "meaning" except it is the "conclusion". You have decided on a conclusion long ago when you were probably too young to have much life experience. If this recent situation is causing you "exaggerated" emotion it is probably because it is time to upgrade your conclusion. It is time to take ourselves into emotional maturity and apply it to those old situations with new eyes. In doing this you are healing your memories. Write down the conclusions you drew and any possible NEW enlightened conclusions you could draw about this old situation. Also apply those to this recent scenario as well.

………………………………………………………………
………………………………………………………………
………………………………………………………………
………………………………………………………………
………………………………………

Once you have replaced some old conclusions with new truths, write down how that makes you feel.

………………………………………………………………
………………………………………………………………
………………………………………………………………
………………………………………

# WORKSHEET 5
## Forgiveness

Now that you have identified your emotions, gotten real about how you feel and transformed some limiting beliefs, you are ready to forgive yourself for ever buying into the misinterpretations that have caused you pain.

We need to forgive ourselves for ever abandoning what we feel and allowing others to get between us and our beloved soul guidance.

If we would have known better we would have done better. Now you know better and you can forgive the parts of yourself that ever gave power to an external authority over your own heart.

The times that we know better but can not do better are our indication of unhealed emotion.

Write down a resent situation where you may have chosen someone else's needs over your own. When you may have abandoned your own instinct.

............................................................
............................................................
..............................

Why did you feel it was better to forgo your instinct?
............................................................
............................................................
..............................

When you ignored your own instinct how did that make you feel?
............................................................
............................................................
..............................

If you would have known that it was safe to follow what your inner guidance was telling you regardless of the fear or doubt, what would you have done instead?
............................................................
............................................................
............................................................
..................

Now go back into that recent situation and choose YOU. Follow what your inner instinct (not fear) is telling you. What does that look like? What are the fears/ emotions that are coming up? Sit with that and watch the situation unfold. Write down what you see happening if you would have chosen to listen to that inner nudge knowing that it is the best choice for you.

..................................................................................
..................................................................................
..................................................................................
..................................................................................
..................................................................................
...............

How does this alternative outcome make you feel?

..................................................................................
..................................................................................
.................................................

What does the new outcome look like?

..................................................................................
..................................................................................
.........................................

You are probably feeling pretty free and satisfied. Your emotions got explored, acknowledged, listened to and validated. You don't really need the validation from the other person. When we focus on others opinions we deny our own internal self validation. This self validation is what we are always looking for and just don't know it. Now that you have seen and felt a new way, it is time to forgive the old way. Please write down a statement of forgiveness to yourself. An example is "I forgive myself for buying into the misbelief that someone else's needs, opinion of me or desire is more important than my inner guidance system. The truth is, my soul knows exactly what I need in order to feel happy and free." When you write this statement, really take it in. When we forgive ourselves for doing the best we could do, we open the space to integrate our new wisdom.

...................................................................................
...................................................................................
...................................................................................
...................................................................................
..................

Each time we go back to our old ways or those old limiting beliefs creep in we can forgive ourselves for any and all judgment of ourselves. We will slip, that is normal. The more forgiveness and love we give to ourself in each moment is what keeps us moving forward and connected to the flow of our own wisdom. How we lovingly relate to ourselves is what keeps our connection to our inner guidance. If you constantly ignore or yell at a child, they will grow to stop trusting you or listening to you over time. This in essence is what our inner guidance does. It may take some practice and consistency with treating ourselves with kindness when we fall and love ourselves when we forget. Eventually you will notice positive shifts, mini miracles that reflect to you your inner work.

# WORKSHEET 6
## Building Trust & Surrender

Let's take a look down memory lane. Now that we have identified our feelings and seen new possibilities, we can apply that to our entire life. We can "choose" how we want to feel by choosing our thoughts. When we look for an alternative perception we are opening ourselves up to experience a different emotion. You may ask "which perception is the truth"? Which thought is the correct and accurate thought? We can think in alignment with fear or with love. Love is the way to your higher self and finding what is "right" for you is your practice of self love. In my opinion, the right thing to do is the loving thing. The wrong thing is what creates more separation and pain. A belief is a thought that we have had over and over again and it becomes a habitual thought which is labeled as a "belief". We change our beliefs by changing our thoughts on a consistent basis.

Now I would like you to look back at your life. Take a situation that continues to be a point of "confusion" for you. "Why did that happen?" "Why did that happen to me?" Why did that happen the way that it happened?" "What was I supposed to learn from that?" "What was I supposed to do or what could I have done to make the outcome more desirable?" Write down what the situation was

..............................................................................
..............................................................................
..............................................................................
..............................................................................
...........................................................................

Now change your language and ask "How did this situation happen FOR me?" Yes thats right, it happened for you. This is a tough one but when you really look at the pain or confusion it caused you, also look at how you have CHANGED because of it. How have you expanded? Did your heart close or open? Everything that happens in our lives is an opportunity for us to grow and expand our idea of things. Did it match your expectation or push you to see how mistakes and messes are perfect too? Maybe your answer is that you are more angry or made bad choices because of it. The only reason these things occur is because we did not see that the situation was happening FOR us in the first place. If you were to see from the beginning that it is happening FOR you, how might you have reacted differently? When I say that it is happening for you, I don't mean that it looks pretty. I mean that there is a bigger plan that is always working on behalf of your deepest desires. Maybe a relationship had to end in order for you to see your own strength. Maybe a job had to be lost for you to step more fully into your power. Does it hurt in the meantime? YES! Does it make you more of who you really wish to be? Eventually. Please write down how you have changed since this difficult situation, "good" or "bad".

...................................................................
...................................................................
...................................................................
...................................................................
...................................................................
...................................................................
...................................................................
...................................................................

Now take a look at your deepest, most honest desires for your life. What is it that you truly want? I ask you this now so that you can see where you are now as apposed to where you WANT to be.

...................................................................
...................................................................
...................................................................
...................................................................
...................................................................

When we look at how we want our life to be, it always has to do with HOW WE WANT TO FEEL. I want this _____ so that I can feel this _____. I encourage you to look back now at this old situation that caused you pain or confusion. If you see that it is or was happening for you and hold that belief, you will see how good you feel through the process. Look at that time and try to remember what you were thinking at the time. "WHY IS THIS HAPPENING TO ME?" What was your belief about why it was occurring and what it means?

………………………………………………………………………
………………………………………………………………………
………………………………………………………………………
………………………………………………………………………
………………………………………………………………………

You may look back from the place you are at today and see that it was always part of the plan if you could have only seen the future. Can you start to see how nothing was ever happening to you or against you. Nothing that has happened was ever happening out of alignment with your bigger desires. An example of this might be if you needed to move to another state because your job was transferred. Maybe you hated the fact that you had to move. You had amazing friends, a great home and life was set. Then you move and at first it feels foreign, uncomfortable and wrong. I encourage you to see how the new conditions are only conditions. This might be a major opportunity to find your HAPPINESS beyond the conditions of your life. This might be the time when you looked deeper, needed to find yoga or spirituality or meditation. This might be the time you were no longer distracted by your fun surroundings so that you could connect to the inner workings of your own heart. This would seem really difficult and unsupportive but the truth is that it is supporting something you may need to "stretch" into. After a year or so of studying yoga, spirituality and meditation you may meet the love of your life because NOW you are in deeper alignment with yourself and with the person that will be attracted into your life. Please write down WHAT could have been orchestrated on your deeper behalf from this confusing or undesired situation. I am only asking for "possibilities" so that you can start to see that there has always been a guiding light working towards your deepest desires.

................................................................................
................................................................................
................................................................................
................................................................................
................................................................................
................................................................................
................................................................................
................................................................................

You can go through as many past circumstances as you like. Each one will bring you to a place of self forgiveness, deeper understanding and expanded trust. After you go through each individual time in your life where you have previously seen through eyes of confusion, you may wish to do some more forgiveness work. Forgiving yourself for any misinterpretations you may have assumed. We can do this for simple things and deeply profound things. When you get the hang of this process, you may want to apply it to simple things in your childhood. An example is "I remember when I was 5 years old and my Mom didn't buy me the doll I wanted." I felt deeply ignored. I carried that pattern with me for years and developed an over reaction to people when I did't feel heard. By doing some forgiveness work we can see that our Mom never meant to ignore us, she simply thought we already had more than enough dolls. This is a very simple example but it carries a deep pattern within it. When we clear even the most simple misinterpretation and replace it with a loving alternative we can start to see how "nothing was ever done to us BECAUSE OF US. Those times we felt punishment or lack of support or love, that was not because we didn't deserve it, that was only our MISINTERPRETATION." I encourage you to write down some simple misinterpretations you may still carry with you about very simple things. As a reminder, a misinterpretation is anything we still see as happening to us that has made us believe we are unloved, unloveable, unsupported, not listened to and unworthy.

......................................................................
......................................................................
......................................................................
......................................................................
......................................................................
......................................................................

If you can look at any of these situations now and see that someone indeed did do something to you to hurt you, cause you pain or disrupt your life, I encourage you to see how that was not ever really about YOU. When we hurt someone it is because we are hurting. When we sabotage someone it is because we have felt sabotaged. When we take something from someone it is because we feel something was taken from us. I would like you to see that nothing is being done to you because of you, it is done to you because of THEM. This exercise is designed to anchor a sense of "self trust" and compassion. You can believe in yourself and your goodness when you see that nothing is "because of the truth of you". Write down some examples of things that happened "to you" that you still think are your fault or because of your unworthiness.

……………………………………………………………………
……………………………………………………………………
……………………………………………………………………
……………………………………………………………………
……………………………………………………………………

Now write down any time you may have thought about someone and judged them. Think about when you have ever done something to someone else when you haven't felt good, when you have felt insecure, threatened, not good enough or jealous. You didn't do it because of them, you did it because of how you thought they made you feel.  It was an action taken due to your own FEELINGS about YOU.  Write that down.

………………………………………………………………
………………………………………………………………
………………………………………………………………
………………………………………………………………
………………………………………………………………

Write down how you would have acted differently if you had been feeling AMAZING about yourself and your life that day.

………………………………………………………………
………………………………………………………………
………………………………………………………………
………………………………………………………………

Do this process so that you can see that YOU are amazing and you will continue to trust that when you act as if you KNOW that.  When we feel bad about ourselves or don't trust the divine support in our lives, we act from fear, scarcity, doubt and negativity, so do others.  The goal of this worksheet is to help you understand the CHOICE that is always there for you by simply having a shift.  When you remember your true divine nature, you can act from that place and see when others don't.  You can see how everything that happens in life is a reaction from fear or love which comes from remembering who we are or who we have forgotten we are.  When we remember that we are love and we are divine we do things that are beautiful and we see that everything happens right on time.  We can get in the way of this flow when we think and act from forgetfulness, from doubt, from separation.  When we choose to love ourselves no matter what, we engender the support of the universe in all that we do.  This sounds so simple but it is really hard.  It becomes much easier with practice and devotion to our true feelings our true selves and our own power to change anything and everything by LOVING IT ANYWAY.

# Part 3

## Transformation

# Feed The Soul

Self realization comes from seeing our true identity. We are very powerful beings who can be powerful in our doubts and powerful in our beliefs. This is always your choice, but I have seen that once people understand their own truth, they always try and choose in alignment with this awareness. I always start my clients out with a very simple daily practice to begin fueling the soul. You have become aware of the choice you have and because of that you can see the truth that is you. You can synchronize with the universe when you choose to see what is happening through love and choose thoughts and actions that support that. Synchronicity is always happening but you can not see it unless you BE it. The best way to begin this daily reality is to start a daily practice.

# WORKSHEET 7
## Daily Practice

The first thing I do with my clients is to start a word journal. Become conscious of the 'words' you use. Words hold vibration. The universe functions on the highest vibration which is UNCONDITIONAL LOVE. The words we use keep us in sync or out of sync with our highest potential. LOVE is the highest vibrational word. What are some of your regular words that may be taking you out of sync with your higher self? An example is anything negative or unloving. A quick way to raise our vibration is to say a daily affirmation to support your unconditional love and acceptance of your emotions. An example is "Today I choose to love and accept all that I feel in efforts to deeply heal". Create your own affirmation.

………………………………………………………………………
………………………………………………………………………
………………………………………………………………………
………………………………………………………………………
……

Say this affirmation at the start and end of every day. After you have your affirmation, we will combine that will our daily intention. The intention will be your call to the universe. When we set an intention we are telling the universe and our higher self what we want for the day and we are in turn asking for support, guidance and assistance. An example of this is "My intention is to see love in the places that scare me". As we do this we trust in our intention and we surrender to the guidance we can not see but truly believe. What is your intention?

………………………………………………………………………
………………………………………………………………………
………………………………………

# WORKSHEET 8
## Raise your Vibration

Now grab a notepad. Grab one that you can tear the pages out of. You are going to start one of my favorite practices. It is called "notes of freedom". You will rip out three pages. Light a candle if you like, put your hand over your heart and tell yourself that you are blocking out this time right now to hear what your heart wants to say. Start writing as soon as you feel the urge to express and let go. Write for as long as you need. You will start to see a flow and feel a release. As soon as you feel your energy shift you are done. Do not worry about how neat your writing is. The point of this exercise is to release energy and write as an expression of the energy that wants to be released. Take the pages and burn them or tear them up. This is an important step in the precess so that you are truly letting go emotionally and then physically.

Now you have learned how to align with your soul through affirmation, intention and through "notes of freedom" writing. The next daily practice I will introduce you to is "soul seeing". This is one of the most profound exercises. You will look into your own soul. Please stand in front of a mirror. I recommend doing this for a couple of minutes each day. You will stand in front of a mirror and just look into your own eyes. After you grow comfortable with this I would like you to be present with how that made you feel. What emotions came up? You are connecting with your innocence, your true self.

.................................................................................
.................................................................................
.................................................................................
.................................................................................
...........................................................................

This exercise will show you a lot about your current relationship to yourself. It forces you to get honest about how you feel about what you see. After you observe your thoughts and feelings, look into your own eyes again and say "AND, I LOVE YOU ANYWAY."

Over a short amount of time, this practice builds a sense of unconditional self love. By looking at your perceived flaws and loving yourself anyway, you begin to care less and less about external opinions. You are owning your truth and building a solid foundation of authentic confidence.

# Worksheet 9
## Oneness

The exercises described in the book are very simple ways to connect to your higher voice, your love voice. We do this by getting honest, supporting our emotional honesty and allowing it to be heard and expressed. We also have supported our higher voice by identifying the words that are in alignment with our highest truth which is love. And finally we took a look into our own soul. When we connect with ourselves in this way we usually feel some deep emotions that need to be loved and healed back to the wholeness of who we truly are. I have designed a life changing meditation for this very process. I don't want you to start this meditation until you have connected with yourself in the above ways for a few weeks. This meditation has a profound and immediate effect on everyone I have given it to or done it with. You are ready for this meditation when you have accepted that you are your own source of unconditional LOVE. The higher self that you have been looking into, writing for and speaking on behalf of is your soul. The emotions we have need to be acknowledged, heard and cleared. They are the parts of ourselves that need more LOVE, not less. In my experience the most healing source of this love is my own unconditionality towards myself. No matter what I feel I love it ANYWAY. If I feel sad, I love myself anyways. If I feel angry, I love myself anyway. If I feel insecure, I love myself anyway. Now you will experience this on a whole new level. When you are ready I invite you into my LOVE IT ANYWAY meditation.

## LOVE IT ANYWAY

Sit in a comfortable position or lay down and close your eyes.

You will visualize each body part as you say this out loud or internally.

top of my head . . . . "I love you, relax"
forehead . . . . . . . . . "I love you, relax"
eye browns . . . . . . "I love you, relax"
eyelids . . . . . . . . . . "I love you, relax"
cheek bones. . . . . . . "I love you, relax"
nose. . . . . . . . . ….."I love you, relax"
lips . . . . . . . . . . … "I love you, relax"
chin . . . . . . . . . … "I love you, relax"
jaw bones . . . . . . ….."I love you, relax"
front of neck ……….."I love you, relax"
clavicle . . . . . . .. . .."I love you, relax"
chest . . . . . . . . . . .."I love you, relax"
shoulders. . . . . . . …"I love you, relax"
biceps . . . . . . . . …"I love you, relax"
elbows. . . . . . . . ….. "I love you, relax
forearm . . . . . . . …"I love you, relax"

abdomen . . . . . . . . . . . ."I love you, relax"
internal organs. . . . . . . . . ."I love you, relax"
hips . . . . . . . . . . . . . .."I love you, relax"
thighs . . . . . . . . . . . ."I love you, relax"
knees. . . . . . . . . . . . . . "I love you, relax"
shins . . . . . . . . . . . . . . "I love you, relax"
ankles . . . . . . . . . . . . . . "I love you, relax"
top of feet. . . . . . . . . "I love you, relax"
sole of feet . . . . . . . . ."I love you, relax"
back of calfs . . . . . . . . ."I love you, relax"
back of knee . . . . . . . . ."I love you, relax"
back of thigh . . . . . . . . "I love you, relax"
bottom . . . . . . . . . . . . ."I love you, relax"
lower back . . . . . . . . . ."I love you, relax"
mid back . . . . . . . . . . . "I love you, relax"
shoulder blades . . . . . . ."I love you, relax"
back of arms. . . . . . . . ."I love you, relax"
back of neck . . . . . . . . ."I love you, relax"
back of head . . . . . . . . ."I love you, relax"
top of head. . . . . . . . . ."I love you, relax"

Please scan your entire body and see if there is an area that pops out for you that is asking for more love. For me I always receive additional "requests" for love.

Give that to yourself and continue until you feel balanced and complete.

It is normal to experience tears and emotions come forward as we give ourselves our own love. Most of us don't know that we can give ourselves the thing we are continually looking to others for. Self love is extremely healing. The day I began this practice I started to see many of my physical ailments disappear. Our physical body carries symptoms when we need more love not less. This is your invitation to give yourself PERMISSION to love yourself as much as you need and as often as you want. This may be the answer to all that you need, it was for me. As soon as we begin these simple practices we are living in a new way. You will see life differently but as it was always meant to be seen. You will live life differently, from a place of self care and self validation. All of those behaviors you previously engaged in may drop away. You will start to notice why you did certain habits and how they are no longer necessary. You may notice that you start to talk differently and sound different. Your soul voice is being heard for maybe the first time! You are being heard by YOU.

When you start to do this work, you will start to see that everyone is just a reflection of you. If everyone is a reflection of you than all you have really ever been doing is trying to get YOU to give yourself LOVE AND ATTENTION. Once you do this you may see "everything" in a much more loving way. You are empowered! You are giving yourself your power back. You may start to see that it was never TAKEN but instead GIVEN. You did not know how to KEEP your power but now you do. You keep it by "Loving yourself anyway".

I encourage you to pass on this invitation by being the example of SELF REALIZATION.

Printed in Great Britain
by Amazon